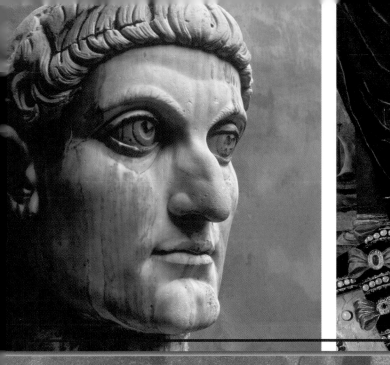

PRIMARY SOURCES OF POLITICAL SYSTEMS™

MONARCHY
A PRIMARY SOURCE ANALYSIS

KATY SCHIEL

rosen central
Primary Source
The Rosen Publishing Group, Inc., New York

Published in 2005 by The Rosen Publishing Group, Inc.
29 East 21st Street, New York, NY 10010

First Edition

Library of Congress Cataloging-in-Publication Data

Schiel, Katy.
Monarchy: a primary source analysis / Katy Schiel.— 1st ed.
        p. cm. — (Primary sources of political systems)
Includes bibliographical references and index.
Contents: Ancient Egypt (3500–30 BC)—Ancient Rome (509 BC–AD 305)—Europe in the Middle Ages (500–1300)—Monarchy in early modern Europe (1400–1750)—Twilight of the monarchy (1789–1918).
ISBN 0-8239-4520-0 (library binding)
1. Monarchy—History. 2. Kings and rulers—History. 3. Divine right of kings.
[1. Monarchy.]
I. Title. II. Series.
JC375.S35 2004
321'.6'09—dc22

2003015896

Manufactured in the United States of America

On the cover: Photograph of the United Kingdom's Queen Elizabeth II addressing members of Parliament on October 29, 1974.

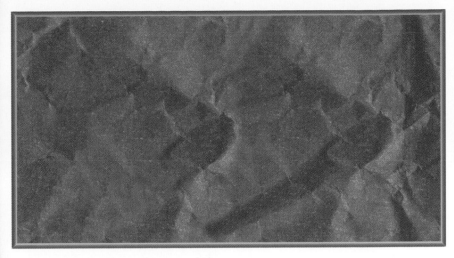

CONTENTS

INTRODUCTION

King, queen, caesar, kaiser, emperor, pharaoh, czar, and monarch are all words that mean the supreme ruler of a nation, territory, or empire. The institution of monarchy, in all its forms, is by far the most ancient of political systems. Nearly every country on earth has been ruled by a monarch—even America!

Monarchy is the political system in which power is vested in one person and is usually passed on through lines of inheritance. The word "monarch" comes from the Greek words for "alone" (*mono*) and "to rule" (*archein*). There are three kinds of monarchies: absolute, limited, and constitutional. Absolute monarchy, the oldest form, has been the most common. An absolute monarch holds complete power over his or her nation and territories. A limited monarch is a ceremonial figurehead who holds no real authority in government. Unlike the absolute monarch, a limited monarch is not above the law. Constitutional monarchy is a form that was popularized in England in the eighteenth century. Under this system, the monarch's powers are limited by the country's constitution and by its legislative body.

This June 4, 2002, photograph shows Great Britain's Queen Elizabeth II leaving Buckingham Palace to attend a ceremony celebrating her fiftieth anniversary as queen. Queen Elizabeth is one of the longest-reigning monarchs in the world today.

Monarchies first developed long before recorded time began. Banding together in small communities, people hunted for food according to the seasons. The first leaders of these groups became monarchs because they were superior hunters who could help save their people from starvation.

Once people learned to plant seeds and harvest food, they began to establish permanent communities across the ancient world. As these communities grew into the first cities, men and women of unique strength and wisdom became the first rulers. We don't know the names of those first kings and queens. They are lost to time and memory.

Early monarchies tended to be ruled by a person who, having inherited his or her position, wielded absolute power. Whenever possible, power was passed to the first-born son.

Through much of early history, a strong monarchy was considered the ideal political system. A powerful king was the glue that held together a society. History has shown that kingdoms ruled by weak monarchs were more likely to experience massive social and political upheaval.

Perhaps the most important idea shared by many early monarchs was the perceived connection between a monarch and the divine. Although the earliest Egyptian pharaohs believed they were actually gods, most monarchs did not usually claim to be gods themselves. Instead, they were God's representatives on earth, given the right to rule by God. Countless kings and queens promoted the idea of the "divine right to rule" to justify the holding of unlimited power. Even today, despotic rulers will claim that God is on their side in order to justify cruel or unfair leadership.

The Egyptian idea of the divine ruler on earth carried over to ancient Greece and was later revived by the Roman emperors. When kings came to the throne in medieval Europe, they were anointed with holy oil as part of their coronation, which was meant to give divine authority to their rule. A coronation is the ceremonial act of crowning a king or queen.

In the early modern period in Europe, monarchs were primarily responsible for creating modern nation states. During the upheavals of this period, the ancient system of absolute monarchy gave way to constitutional monarchy in many places. The monarch's power was greatly reduced, as he or she ruled in conjunction with a legislative assembly that represented members of the general population. By the early twentieth century, most countries had rejected monarchy as a form of government, preferring instead to be ruled by elected leaders who would speak to the people's needs.

CHAPTER ONE

ANCIENT EGYPT (3500–30 BC)

The kings and queens of ancient Egypt are known as pharaohs. They were part of the longest ruling monarchy in history. From about 3500 BC, when the first of the kings ruled over a united Egypt, to 30 BC, when Cleopatra killed herself rather than submit to the rule of Roman conquerors, ancient Egypt flourished under the leadership of the pharaohs. The ancient Egyptian civilization, the oldest known to humankind, is divided into dynasties and periods. A dynasty is the span of time during which all the rulers of a kingdom are from one family or clan.

Cleopatra became queen of Egypt in 51 BC when she was only seventeen years old. She was the last of the pharaohs of ancient Egypt.

The Divine Pharaohs

Ancient Egyptians believed they were ruled for many thousands of years by the gods before the first pharaoh, Narmer, came to the throne. All pharaohs were considered to be divine, because they were believed to have descended directly from the gods. Because the pharaohs were thought to be divine, they possessed absolute power.

As the representative of the gods on earth, the pharaoh was a visible symbol of divine authority and, in theory, was the only landholder, priest, and judge. He presided over the most important religious ceremonies, dedicated building projects, decided government policy, supervised officials, and stored grain to use during times of bad harvest. He also ensured that the kingdom's history was preserved and honored, and he commanded the army in war.

In practice, however, the pharaoh had a lot of help running the kingdom. Typically, a vizier, or chief minister, oversaw all administrative functions. This person, usually a man, answered to no one but the pharaoh. In some cases, he also supervised the priesthood or the military. When he did not, high priests and military leaders ranked directly below the pharaoh. Various senior and midlevel officials called *imy-ra*, or overseers, reported to the vizier. These overseers—and in some cases the vizier—monitored the nomarchs, or governors of local provinces who made or administered policies covering the average laborer.

Pharaohs had traditional authority, which means that their power was accepted on the basis of long-standing custom. The average Egyptian accepted the notion of the pharaoh's divinity. Nevertheless,

MESOPOTAMIAN KINGS

In 3500 BC, the two kingdoms of Egypt were united by Narmer, the legendary first pharaoh. Around the same time in Mesopotamia (present-day Iraq), other civilizations, including the Assyrians, Sumerians, and Babylonians, began to flourish under a series of efficient monarchs. Gilgamesh, one of the first and most famous of the Mesopotamian kings, ruled much later in 2700 BC. During Egypt's long golden age, many other monarchies grew and flourished as other civilizations developed near Egypt. Greece, Rome, Syria, Persia, and Phoenicia all became powerful and established monarchies while Egypt's pharaohs reigned.

This stone relief from the eighth century BC portrays Gilgamesh holding a lion that he has captured. It was found among the ruins of the palace of Sargon II in Khorsabad, Iraq, in 1843 by French archaeologist Paul-Emile Botta.

pharaohs often fortified their positions by filling all key administrative and military positions with trustworthy members of the royal family. Moreover, a pharaoh's authority could also have been strengthened by a reputation as a strong military leader or for leading the kingdom through a crisis, such as a drought.

The Egyptian monarchy was not always strong. Like every administration, it had its good and bad times. Until the fourth dynasty (2550 BC), pharaonic power enjoyed its golden age. The throne began to lose its power very slowly until it was overtaken by the Romans in 30 BC.

Ancient Artifacts: A Window into Egypt's Rulers

Most of what we know about ancient Egypt and its rulers comes from countless discoveries of artifacts from the period. The Palermo Stone, the Palette of Narmer, and *The Admonitions of an Egyptian Sage* are three of the most significant finds. They highlight the importance of the monarch in ancient Egyptian civilization.

The Palermo Stone

One important source of our knowledge about ancient Egypt is the Palermo Stone. It is a fragment from a large basalt stone tablet inscribed with the names of the early monarchs. Created around 3000 BC, the Palermo Stone is inscribed on both sides with the earliest times of royal history.

Until 3500 BC, the area we now know as Egypt was actually two separate kingdoms. The southern half was known as Upper Egypt and the northern part was Lower Egypt. The Palermo Stone recorded the history of the kings of Lower Egypt, beginning with the thousands of years in which Egypt was believed to have been ruled by the gods. The history covers the time of the god Horus, who is said to have given the throne to the human king Narmer. Human rulers are listed up to the fifth dynasty. The last name preserved on the stone is that of Neferirkare. He was the third of the nine kings of the fifth dynasty (2465–2325 BC). The Palermo Stone is a very important document in Egyptian history because it reveals the names of Egypt's early rulers. It has helped historians find their way through the long maze of Egyptian history.

The Palette of Narmer

The Palette of Narmer was discovered in 1898 by British archaeologist J. E. Quibell in the ancient predynastic capital Hierakonpolis. Unfortunately, the exact circumstances of the find were not recorded, which adds to its mystery. What archaeologists do know is that this flat slab of slate, measuring twenty-five inches (sixty-four centimeters) high, is carved on both sides with depictions of events and symbols from the reign of King Narmer. Most historians believe that it dates from about 3050 to 3000 BC.

Like many artifacts from ancient Egypt, there is much about the Palette of Narmer that is shrouded in mystery. It might only be a slate palette meant for preparing cosmetics, decorated with symbols representing the legendary first king of Egypt, Narmer, and the unification of Upper and Lower Egypt.

However, the substantial weight and decoration of the Palette of Narmer suggest it had more important uses. Narmer wears the

The Palette of Narmer, shown above, illustrates events from the reign of Narmer. The central image on the front of the palette *(left)* shows two men taming wild animals by tying their stretched necks together. This symbolizes the unification of Upper and Lower Egypt. The central image on the back of the palette *(right)* shows Narmer inspecting beheaded corpses, which likely represent enemies slain in battle.

crown of Upper Egypt on one side of the palette and the crown of Lower Egypt on the other. This may indicate that he was the king responsible for the merging of Upper and Lower Egypt into a single kingdom.

Pharaoh Mentuhotep II reunited Egypt after it had been divided by conquest and internal strife for more than a century. Mentuhotep II launched many building projects, the most notable of which is his burial complex that houses this statue.

As we learned from the Palermo Stone, the ancient Egyptians believed that the gods ruled Egypt for many thousands of years before the god Horus is said to have given the throne to Narmer. Egyptian tradition credits Narmer as the king who united the two Egypts.

The Admonitions of an Egyptian Sage

The Admonitions of an Egyptian Sage are the lamentations of an Egyptian wise man called Ipuwer. It is written on papyrus, an early kind of paper. Dating from about 2200 BC, the narration describes a very bleak time during the first intermediary period of Egypt. Part of the "dark ages" in Egyptian history, this period began in 2180 BC and lasted for about a century.

In *The Admonitions of an Egyptian Sage*, Ipuwer laments an almost complete breakdown of the long-established social order and calls for the restoration of a powerful monarchy. He paints a horrific scene of mummies speaking from the grave and dead bodies floating down the Nile. There is political unrest across the land, and people no longer feel safe. Ancient documents are being destroyed, and monuments are being smashed. Foreigners have invaded Egypt, and there is no strong leader who can put an end to the suffering and chaos. Ipuwer complains that "hearts are violent, pestilence is throughout the land, blood is everywhere, death is not lacking, and the mummy-cloth speaks even before one comes near it . . . noblemen are in distress, while the poor man is full of joy." To Ipuwer, the health of the monarchy reflected the health of the society and was the only guarantee of civilization.

The End of the Egyptian Monarchy

Around 2055 BC, the throne of the pharaoh was restored to its former glory by Pharaoh Mentuhotep II. Despite many periods of change that sometimes interrupted Egypt's independence, pharaohs continued to rule and flourish up until the reign of Cleopatra in the first century BC. Legend has it that rather than submit to the foreign rule of the Romans, Cleopatra killed herself by allowing a poisonous snake to bite her. The great reign of the pharaohs was over, and Egypt became a part of the Roman Empire.

CHAPTER TWO

ANCIENT ROME (509 BC–AD 305)

According to ancient history, the city of Rome was founded in 753 BC (about 3,000 years after the beginning of Egypt's monarchy). Rome's earliest rulers were kings. Romulus was first. In 509 BC, Tarquin the Proud, the seventh king of Rome, became the last. The despised Tarquin was deposed for his cruelty. Fearing the unlimited power of kings, the people of Rome established a new form of government called a republic. A republic is a political structure in which supreme power is held not by a monarch but by the citizens who exercise their power through the officers and representatives they elect. The Roman Republic lasted 500 years.

Octavian was the first monarch of the Roman Empire. Officially, his title was princeps, or first citizen, not emperor.

This undated copper engraving depicts the Roman Senate in session. The Senate formed the main governing body of the Roman Republic and held considerable clout. It appointed the consuls and had the power to nominate a dictator in times of emergencies. The Senate lost much of its real power during the Roman Empire.

The Republic

At the head of the Roman Republic were two consuls who shared equal power. They controlled the army, made laws, and set taxes. The consuls, who were elected every year, were advised by the Senate, which was made up of men from Rome's wealthiest families. Most of the time, the consuls followed the Senate's advice.

Below the senators were prefects and tribunes. Prefects ran the day-to-day operations of the city, such as the markets and ports. Some even heard court cases. In theory, tribunes spoke for the poor, and they could veto, or block, any measure that the Senate voted for that affected the poor.

At the bottom of the political structure was the assembly, which was made up of all free males who were Roman citizens. The assembly elected the consuls, prefects, senators, and tribunes. However, it was set up in such a way that the votes of the rich carried more weight than those of the poor. Accordingly, policies tended to favor the wealthy. Moreover, women, noncitizens, and slaves had no votes.

Downfall of the Republic

The Roman Republic was designed to stop a single ruler from ever growing powerful again. However, this arrangement did not always work out. By 31 BC, Rome was at the center of an enormously rich empire that stretched across Europe and the Middle East. However, the republican government that had worked well while Rome was a small city proved inadequate for a sprawling empire. Quarrels among rival senators led to a breakdown in the 500-year-old republic. Military leaders such as Julius Caesar (100–44 BC) began to demand more political power. Caesar was murdered in 44 BC by a group of senators who feared that he intended to establish a monarchy and make himself king. Caesar's murder demonstrated the extent of the Romans' hatred for the very idea of monarchy. Although the senators murdered Caesar, the political problems in Rome continued.

In 43 BC, Caesar's nephew, Octavian, forced the Senate to make him consul. In 31 BC, he declared himself "first citizen" of Rome and made the Senate give him the powers of a tribune for life. With control of the army and veto power over the Senate, he had become, in effect, a king. In 27 BC, Octavian became emperor, renaming himself Augustus. The age of the Roman monarch had begun. This new breed of emperor who ruled in conjunction with the Senate became the model and envy of later European kings.

Constantine I (Constantine the Great) ruled the Roman Empire between AD 306 and 337. His reign was marked by great military victories and territorial expansion. He is perhaps best known for being the first Roman emperor to endorse Christianity. This statue of his head dates from around 325.

The Roman Empire

The Roman Empire lasted for five centuries, during which it passed through various phases of development, crisis, and recovery. Although in theory the emperors ruled in collaboration with the Senate, they almost always had absolute power and could force their wills on the Senate. Accordingly, the empire often reflected the personalities and interests of the emperors.

Nevertheless, many emperors lived in constant fear for their lives. They often went to great lengths to protect themselves, including ordering the death of people they distrusted. Perhaps the most notorious of the emperors was Caligula, who reigned between AD 37 and 41. He executed senators and other rich citizens whom he disliked or of whom he was suspicious. Widely regarded as having been insane, Caligula was eventually assassinated by a group of soldiers.

The empire was most successful when the emperor was a strong, organized leader. A good emperor was usually someone who commanded respect for his military prowess, his organization of the bureaucracy, and his development of public works, such as roads, stadiums, and bridges. Such an emperor was also perceived as having a general sense of fairness in terms of taxes and the treatment of other government officials, especially the senators.

The Golden Age of Rome

Under Emperor Trajan, who ruled from AD 98 to 117, the Roman Empire expanded to its largest size. From modern Portugal in the west to modern Kuwait in the east and from the British Isles in the north to modern Sudan in the south, the Roman Empire was the largest empire in history, and the emperor was placed firmly at the top.

Emperor Trajan was perhaps the most beloved and able of the Roman emperors. He was said to have a majestic and grand appearance. Despite his iron will, he was reported to be extremely kind and chivalrous. He was famous for his compassionate treatment of the poor. During his reign, the Roman Empire conquered many lands

Emperor Trajan *(inset)* erected this building around the turn of the second century AD on the Isle of Philae in Egypt. At the time, Egypt was part of the Roman Empire. Known as the Kiosk of Trajan, the structure includes sculptures portraying Trajan as a pharaoh making offerings to various Egyptian gods, including Isis and Horus.

and established many settlements. Along with the new Roman communities came order, especially to the Germanic areas to the north, which were regarded as uncivilized.

Trajan was also a great builder, as evidenced by the many ruins of his public buildings. In addition, he encouraged commerce and industry within the empire. Art and culture flourished during his rule. His legacy can be compared to those of the most enlightened monarchs of the later Italian Renaissance.

Emperor Trajan's rule represents the golden age of Rome, a time when there were no military defeats, culture flourished, and the emperor was the supreme leader of 20 million residents throughout the great empire.

Hadrian's Wall

One of the greatest symbols of the power and reach of the Roman emperors still stands in Great Britain. Hadrian's Wall, built in AD 122, runs across 73 miles (118 kilometers) of open English countryside, separating the north of Great Britain from the south.

Hadrian became emperor when Trajan died of a stroke in AD 117. Hadrian, who had his own ideas about the empire, did not want to conquer any new territories. But the army, which was used to being at war, was unhappy with this new policy. In addition, Hadrian, who did not get along with many of the senators, had some of them executed. He became extremely unpopular.

One of Hadrian's favorite and most often repeated sayings was, "A ruler exists for the State and not the State for the ruler." To this end, Hadrian improved communications within the empire and created an international civil service to administer the community of nations within the Roman Empire. The Roman Empire was at its greatest size and power. The soldiers needed a bold and grand project to keep them busy and useful. Hadrian knew just what to do.

The British Isles had been more or less under Rome's control since 55 BC, when Julius Caesar invaded the southern coast. After almost 200 years, however, Rome had still failed to conquer the

Hadrian's Wall ran 73 miles (118 km) and was more than 16 feet (5 m) high. It formed the northern boundary of the Roman Empire under Hadrian. The garrisons that were located a mile apart along the wall allowed the Romans to monitor the movement of goods, people, and animals across the frontier.

fierce and defiant Celts of the Scottish north. In AD 122, Hadrian visited Britain and ordered a wall to be built between the Solway Firth in the west and the River Tyne in the east. The wall would separate Romans from people they considered to be barbarians.

Roman soldiers built the great wall over six years. In addition to being able fighting men, these soldiers were often skilled architects, masons, carpenters, and surveyors whose talents are apparent today. The wall is ten feet (three meters) wide with milecastles, or garrisons, at every mile. Thousands of soldiers were positioned at the wall,

Marcus Aurelius was very pious and committed to a system of beliefs known as Stoicism. Stoicism stressed self-discipline, simplicity, virtue, and inner tranquility. Marcus Aurelius wrote about Stoicism throughout his reign. A collection of these writings, *The Meditations of Marcus Aurelius*, has become a classic of Western literature.

keeping watch over windswept and isolated Scotland.

To the "barbarians" of the north, Hadrian's Wall must have seemed an awesome symbol of the strength of the Roman emperor. Even today, the wall remains one of the most spectacular symbols of how far the Roman Empire reached.

Marcus Aurelius

When he was only a child, Marcus Aurelius attracted the attention of Emperor Hadrian, who appointed the young man to the priesthood. He became emperor in AD 161 and ruled until AD 180. Marcus Aurelius Antoninus Augustus was the only Roman emperor besides Julius Caesar whose writings have become classics of Western literature. Although far from a remarkable warrior or administrator, he was well loved by his people because of his compassion. Marcus Aurelius was a social reformer who worked for the betterment of the poor, slaves, and criminals.

CHAPTER THREE

EUROPE IN THE MIDDLE AGES (500–1300)

The story of monarchy in the Middle Ages revolves around the consolidation of land into the first nation-states. The Middle Ages was a period of European history between the fall of the Roman Empire around AD 476 and about the middle of the fifteenth century.

The Feudal System

At the beginning of the Middle Ages, Europe as we know it today did not exist. Rather, it was an enormous collection of small areas ruled by lords under the feudal system. The structure of the feudal system resembled the

This detail from an illustration depicts the coronation of Charlemagne by Pope Leo III. During the Middle Ages, the church played an important role in advancing the notion that monarchs ruled by divine right.

This fifteenth-century painting depicts peasants tilling and sowing a field in the shadow of the Louvre, the royal palace of King Charles V in Paris, France. The painting is from a larger collection called *Les Tres Riche Heures* (The Very Rich Hours), which was painted by brothers Paul, Hermann, and Jean Limbourg.

shape of a pyramid. A mass of serfs at the base worked to produce wealth for the small number of lords above them. Serfs were bound to the manor and could not leave it or marry without the manor lord's permission. Serfs, who were uneducated, did all the work on the manor farm. They had small plots of land they could work for themselves. Sometimes a serf could earn enough money to buy his freedom.

A lord, or vassal, ruled lands granted to him by his king. These lands were called fiefs. Within a fief, a vassal could give portions of his land to vassals of his own. Someone could have been the vassal of one person but the lord of another.

At the top of the pyramid sat the monarch who reaped the wealth created by the serfs below. In return, the monarch provided military protection from outside invaders. This was a very convenient and lucrative system for the medieval monarchs because it provided them with easy access to wealth and power. Monarchs justified their positions by claiming to possess the divine right to rule bestowed upon them by God. The monarchies of the Middle Ages were the force behind the emergence of the modern nation-state, which came into being at the end of the medieval period.

But dynasties came and went quite often, and hereditary power could not be assumed. Establishing legitimacy was a major concern for monarchs. King John of England, for example, failed to establish a strong rule and lost much of his power.

Charlemagne

One monarch whose legitimacy was unquestioned was Charlemagne, who reigned from 768 to 814. He was known in his lifetime as the father of Europe. A Frankish (present-day German) king, Charlemagne was a great patron of artists and scholars. He rescued from oblivion much of the ancient learning of Greece and Rome. He was perhaps the first great monarch of the Middle Ages.

Charlemagne, having converted from paganism to Christianity very early in life, made it his mission to convert the rest of Europe. This was often a brutal and bloody process. A brilliant and ruthless fighter, Charlemagne was the first monarch since the fall of the Roman Empire strong enough to unite the lands of western Europe, which had spent the previous 400 years in chaos. He was also able to create the structure for Europe that we know today.

On Christmas Day in 800, as Charlemagne prayed in Saint Peter's Cathedral in Rome, Pope Leo III placed a golden crown on his bowed head, crowning him king of the Holy Roman Empire. This coronation established the legitimacy of Charlemagne's dynasty, which lasted for the next 150 years.

Throughout the Middle Ages, Charlemagne was considered a model for Christian rulers. His reign was marked by the consolidation of Christian Europe and significant advances in education, law, government, and religion. This golden bust of Charlemagne was created around 1350 to store fragments of the emperor's skull.

William the Conqueror

After the rule of Charlemagne, it took 200 years for another great monarch to arise in Europe. This was William the Conqueror. Invading England in 1066, William the Conqueror had himself crowned king on Christmas Day. Although it took until 1072 for him to take over the entire area of Britain, he used force and clever planning to establish his legitimacy and strengthen his monarchy.

William's invasion of England in 1066 is a pivotal moment in history, and the famous Bayeux Tapestry tells its story. A 230-foot (70 m) long strip of linen embroidered with battle scenes and Latin words, the Bayeux Tapestry describes in pictures William the Conqueror's victory at the Battle of Hastings. In 1066, the Normans (descendants of the Vikings who lived in what is now France), led by Duke William, crossed the English Channel and conquered all of England in one vicious battle. William, now called the conqueror,

The Bayeux Tapestry is an account of William the Conqueror's invasion of England. This detail from the tapestry portrays the construction of a fortified military camp at Hastings. Despite its name, the Bayeux Tapestry is actually embroidery on eight long strips of bleached linen. The tapestry, as it exists today, measures 230 feet (70 m) long and 20 inches (51 cm) tall.

was determined to establish successful control of England. He realized that in order to be accepted as England's legitimate monarch, he would have to respect the laws and traditions of his new people. By skillfully blending new laws with the traditional laws and customs, William was able to convince the conquered Anglo-Saxons to accept him as the legitimate monarch of England. He allowed villages and manors to retain a good deal of autonomy in exchange for military service and monetary payments. This brand of feudalism was seen as an excellent way to strengthen the monarchy. As Britain's first Norman king, William laid the groundwork for Britain's future economic and political success. Always ready for a fight, William was killed in battle in 1087.

Eleanor of Aquitaine

Another strong monarch who ruled both England and France in the Middle Ages was Eleanor of Aquitaine. Ruling from 1122 to 1204, Eleanor was one of the most powerful personalities of the Middle Ages. Eleanor became heir to the vast area of France known as Aquitaine when she was a young girl. At age fifteen, she married the gloomy and severe Louis VII of France, adding large amounts of land to their French holdings. At age nineteen, she offered Bernard of Clairvaux thousands of her vassals to fight in the Second Crusade. Legend states that she appeared at Vézelay Cathedral on a white horse. Dressed for battle, she urged the crowds to join the Crusades. While Bernard was happy for her support, he was less than pleased that she planned to have 300 of her ladies-in-waiting accompany her. Although Eleanor made it to Jerusalem and back, the pope forbade women from ever participating in the Crusades again.

Eleanor and Louis VII's time together during the Second Crusade proved that they were not well matched, and the marriage was annulled on a technicality. Eleanor's land reverted to her control.

In 1154, Eleanor married Henry, Duke of Normandy (later King Henry II of England). She bore Henry eight children, two of whom later became kings. Together Eleanor and Henry built an impressive empire through well-crafted alliances, strong military command, and family connections.

Even in her old age, Eleanor always traveled. Moving through the kingdoms of Europe, she often risked her life traveling through dangerous areas to maintain the loyalty of her subjects, to form marriage alliances, and to manage her army and estates. In her old age, Eleanor became known as the grandmother of Europe.

This is the tomb of Eleanor of Aquitaine. Eleanor was a very ambitious woman. She spent sixteen years in prison for conspiring with two of her sons to overthrow their father. Although not technically a queen, Eleanor ruled England between 1189 and 1199 with the permission of her son King Richard the Lionheart.

The Magna Carta

While monarchs were the absolute rulers of their kingdoms, there were times when their subjects rose up against them to question their claim of divine rule. King John of England, grandson of Eleanor of Aquitaine, was considered an unjust and greedy ruler, mostly because of his excessive use of taxes to fund the Third Crusade.

A TROUBADOUR SINGS PRAISES FOR ELEANOR

Eleanor was a great patron of the arts, especially music, and she helped to popularize the medieval concept of courtly love. Her grandfather was William IX of Aquitaine, one of the first known troubadours in history. Her support of the medieval troubadour tradition helped place it firmly in the aristocratic courts of France. Eleanor of Aquitaine is an excellent example of the enlightened monarch who used her power to advance culture during the Middle Ages.

The verses of troubadours ranked among the most popular forms of entertainment in the royal courts of the Middle Ages.

In addition, his barons saw him as weak and sneaky, and he fought continuously with his family.

In 1215, a rebellious group of barons took up arms against King John and presented a list of demands that would limit his authority. King John reluctantly signed this list to make peace, but he did not keep his word. The result was civil war in England, during which he was killed. The document, however, which became known as the Magna Carta, or "great charter," is considered one of the cornerstones of the concept of liberty, as it is understood today.

The Magna Carta contained several important elements. It gave the Church of England the final word on the selection of people for powerful positions. It prevented a king from demanding more than a reasonable amount of money to run the government without the consent of feudal tenants. Most important, the Magna Carta gave to the nobility the power to limit the king's actions through the use of a written grant. And it gave people the right to a fair trial.

Drafted and signed nearly 800 years ago, the Magna Carta is still considered one of the most influential documents in world history. It includes many concepts of civil liberties that are the cornerstones of modern democracies. These include the right to a speedy and public trial by an impartial jury and the idea that no one, including heads of government, is above the rule of law. Refer to page 57 for a partial transcription.

CHAPTER FOUR

MONARCHY IN EARLY MODERN EUROPE (1400–1750)

In Europe, the period between 1400 and 1750 is often called monarchy's golden age. During this time, the institution of monarchy was remarkably strong. The Renaissance in Italy saw a flowering of culture and art unparalleled in history, largely financed by its monarchs. Other European monarchs were establishing colonies in far corners of the globe.

Monarchy in Italy

At the end of the end of the Middle Ages, Italy was enjoying a rebirth of art and culture known as the Renaissance. During the Renaissance, Florence was a

This is the throne room of Emperor Napoléon I at Fontainebleau château in Fontainebleau, France. The throne room is the place where monarchs officially accept visitors. It is typically the most elaborately decorated room of a palace.

hotbed of culture, with some of the most talented artists and musicians of the era making their homes there. Artists and thinkers such as Leonardo da Vinci and Michelangelo produced history-changing works under the patronage of the Italian monarchs.

The Medicis were a family of Italian bankers who came to the Italian monarchy around 1434. Although they were powerful monarchs, they also had a strong family tradition of artistic patronage and talent.

Lorenzo de' Medici

Lorenzo de' Medici (1449–1492), or Lorenzo the Magnificent, was a statesman, ruler, and patron of the arts. Among his many

Lorenzo de' Medici came to power in Italy when he was just twenty years old. In addition to his patronage of the arts, he started an impressive collection of books from around the world. He established a workshop to copy the books so their knowledge would be spread throughout Europe.

contributions to Florentine culture was the generous support he gave to Leonardo da Vinci and Michelangelo. The great Italian writer Niccolò Machiavelli called Lorenzo de' Medici "the greatest patron of literature and art that any prince has ever been." In his highly influential treatise *The Prince*, Machiavelli used Lorenzo as the perfect example of a strong leader.

MACHIAVELLI'S *THE PRINCE*

One of the most influential supporters of the idea of an unlimited, absolute monarchy was Niccolò Machiavelli. In *The Prince* (1513), Machiavelli argues that unity and peace can be achieved only under the rule of a single leader with enough power to suppress local unrest and partisan squabbling. This ruler must also be cunning and determined enough to keep his position strong, no matter what conspires to bring him down. This is an example of realpolitik, a policy based on keeping power rather than pursuing ideals. Although *The Prince* was written in response to what was happening in Italy during Machiavelli's lifetime, it has nonetheless become the bible for absolutist systems.

Niccolò Machiavelli

England's Monarchy

During the sixteenth and seventeenth centuries, the English monarchy saw both the expansion of its power with the long and prosperous reign of Queen Elizabeth I (ruled 1558–1603) and the contraction of its power with the beheading of Charles I for treason in 1649. Constitutional monarchy was finally established in England with the Glorious Revolution of 1688.

The Execution of Charles I

Unlucky Charles I of England, who reigned from 1625 to 1649, was a strong believer in absolute monarchy and in his own divine right to rule. These beliefs had been passed down to him through his family and from history. But unlike his predecessors, Charles was not allowed to get away with his very undemocratic actions.

Elizabeth I is widely regarded as one of England's most powerful and successful monarchs. During her reign, England increased its colonial holdings and its stature as a world power. Elizabeth I also presided over the establishment of the Church of England, which quieted religious antagonism between Catholics and Protestants.

Beginning in 1629, Charles I was engaged in a drawn-out conflict with the British Parliament. This dispute resulted in a civil war that

BOSSUET AND THE DIVINE RIGHT OF KINGS

One of the main theorists of divine right monarchy in the seventeenth century was the French theologian and court preacher Bishop Jacques-Bénigne Bossuet (1627–1704). In his book *Politics Drawn from the Very Words of Holy Scripture*, Bossuet argues that government was ordained from God so humans could live in a regulated, organized society. He argued that since God established kings and reigned through them, monarchy was the most ancient, most natural, and most desirable form of government. And since kings received their power from God, their authority and power were absolute. They were responsible to God alone and not to parliaments. Since only God could appoint kings, Bossuet wrote, "It appears from this that the person of kings is sacred, and to move against them is sacrilege. God causes them to be anointed by the prophets with a sacred unction, as He caused the pontiffs and His altars to be anointed."

started in 1642. During the war, Charles I was captured and put on trial in 1649. He was accused of being a traitor and a tyrant. Even during the trial, Charles refused to take his hat off before the judges, reinforcing their perception of him as an arrogant tyrant. He was found guilty.

Before his execution in 1649, Charles addressed the crowd, saying, "I have delivered to my conscience; I pray God you do take those

This is the death warrant for King Charles I. It was signed by fifty-nine of the sixty-seven judges of the High Court of Justice who tried him for treason. Thirty-three witnesses from all walks of life testified against him. The warrant was issued on January 29, 1649. It was addressed specifically to three officers, two of whom refused to participate in the execution of the king. Refer to page 57 for a transcription.

courses that are best for the good of the kingdom and your own salvation." With those words, Charles became the first and only English monarch beheaded for treason.

English Monarchy Is Abolished and Restored

Only seven days after the execution of Charles I, the institution of monarchy was abolished in England. Parliament determined that the office of the king in England was unnecessary, burdensome, and dangerous to the liberty, society, and public interest of the people. The Council of State was set up, with Oliver Cromwell as its leader.

But the monarchy could not be destroyed so easily. When Charles II returned from exile to become king of England in 1660, during what is now known as the Restoration, the judges who had signed his father's death warrant were tried as regicides (murderers of a king) and executed. The monarchy was now safely back in control. However, its powers were to be permanently lessened in 1688 when the Glorious Revolution established a constitutional monarchy.

Louis XIV of France

In France, Louis XIV, who ruled from 1643 to 1715, became the model and envy of other European monarchs. During his long reign, Louis XIV established nearly absolute control of the government and church. Kings and queens in Spain, Austria, Russia, and Prussia, from around 1650 to the early nineteenth century, all tried to follow his lead. Frederick the Great of Prussia (reigned 1740–1786) and Catherine the Great of Russia (reigned 1762–1796) were strong rulers. But they failed to equal Louis XIV in power.

Versailles During the Reign of Louis XIV

If one building symbolizes the grandeur and decadence of absolute monarchy, it is the Palace of Versailles in France. It was built by the the Sun King, Louis XIV of France. Louis XIV, who had inherited an extremely prosperous country, was able to grasp minute details of the nature of kingship. No other monarch in history has understood as well the symbolic functions of being a king. The foundation of his system was to make a distinction between real power and ceremonial grandeur.

The Palace of Versailles was originally a hunting lodge until King Louis XIV expanded it into an opulent palace beginning in 1669. It was the official royal residence between 1682 and 1790. Historians estimate that maintaining the palace during this period consumed up to 25 percent of France's national income. This photograph, taken between 1890 and 1900, shows the palace's Gallery of Mirrors.

Instead of giving his ministers real power, he granted them symbolic power that depended on his final word. Denying the nobles of actual power, he instead accorded them endless decorative honors to give the illusion of worth and significance. This kept the nobility quite busy while the king held all of the true power. Louis XIV is famous for saying "L'etat c'est moi," meaning "I am the state," which sums up how he felt about his position.

When he assumed power at age twenty-three, he shocked the world by declaring that he would rule France alone.

Louis hated Paris, preferring to live at the Palace of Versailles, an opulent palace that housed his entire court. At Versailles, etiquette and the pleasure of the king ruled above all else. French nobles and courtiers were expected to come to Versailles to await passing glances from the king. Louis, who had a phenomenal memory, complained if he did not see someone in attendance. Versailles had countless galleries, but nobles were forbidden from discussing politics since informers haunted the halls.

Lavish and time-consuming formalities—hunting, masked balls, and billiards—filled the days and nights of the court of Versailles. In this way, Louis was able to keep the well-educated but powerless elites at his mercy during his fifty-five-year reign. His descendants, however, were not so lucky. Louis XVI and his wife, Marie Antoinette, reigned during a much more dangerous time for the monarchy—a time of new ideas that challenged the monarchs' divine right to rule.

CHAPTER FIVE

TWILIGHT OF THE MONARCHY (1789–1918)

The institution of monarchy, with a few exceptions (ancient Greece being one), had long been seen as a divine institution not to be questioned by ordinary people. In the eighteenth century, that belief was turned upside down. Free-thinking men and women in the American colonies, such as Thomas Paine, were challenging the rule of their monarch, King George III in England. The disastrous rule of Louis XVI in France and the success of the American Revolution propelled the French people to take up arms, ending the life of the king as well as the institution of monarchy—at least for the moment.

Emperor Hirohito was Japan's monarch during World War II. Japan's defeat in the war marked the decline of the Japanese monarchy. Although Hirohito was allowed to remain on the throne, his role and the monarchy in general became symbolic.

The French Revolution

Eventually, the French monarchy ran out of money. Louis XIV had spent a fortune building the Palace of Versailles, Louis XV had wasted millions on his own pleasures, and Louis XVI had given tremendous amounts to help the American colonies fight off the British in the American Revolution.

In 1789, Louis XVI called together the Estates-General for the first time since 1614. He was hoping to raise money. The Estates-General was a ruling body created to represent all the people of France, even the poorest. Members of the First Estate were the clergy. Second Estate members were the nobles. The Third Estate, which made up more than 95 percent of the population, comprised the workers, poor, and oppressed people of France.

When the Estates-General came together, several things happened. Members of the first two estates, who were expecting the king to give them new political power, were furious when Louis XVI announced he was now expecting them to pay taxes. Until that time, only people of the Third Estate had paid taxes to the king. In addition, the nobles and clergy refused to admit representatives of the Third Estate into the meeting. Outraged, members of the Third Estate declared themselves the National Assembly. They met on June 20, 1789, on the tennis court at Versailles, took the Tennis Court Oath, and drew up plans to run a constitutional government.

The Declaration of the Rights of Man

The Declaration of the Rights of Man and of the Citizen was a revolutionary manifesto drafted by Abbé Emmanuel-Joseph Sieyès in

This etching depicts the taking of the Tennis Court Oath by 577 members of France's Third Estate on June 20, 1789. The oath reads in part that the National Assembly "decrees that all members of this Assembly shall immediately take a solemn oath not to separate, and to reassemble wherever circumstances require, until the constitution of the kingdom is established and consolidated upon firm foundations."

1789 and adopted on August 26 of that year by France's National Assembly. Two years later, in 1791, the declaration was attached as the preamble to France's new constitution. It defined a number of inalienable rights to be enjoyed by all men. This revolutionary pronouncement canceled the divine right of kings to rule, which had been the basis for French government and social structure since the Middle Ages.

The seventeen articles of the Declaration of the Rights of Man and of the Citizen, which were adopted by the National Assembly in 1789, formed the preamble of France's first constitution, which was created in 1791. Refer to page 58 for a partial transcription.

Several articles dealt with abolition of the monarchy. Others addressed the rights of the common (white) man to enjoy liberty and security, to own property, and to be free from oppression. Confusion and hysteria became intense. It was clear that the three estates, which had very different ideas and needs, would be unable to agree on guidelines that would benefit everyone. The king could not or did not want to help the groups find common ground. In the end, his disregard for his people set in motion the French Revolution.

Death of Louis XVI

In 1793, four years after the declaration was written and the revolution began, Louis XVI and Queen Marie Antoinette were beheaded on the guillotine. It was a huge turning point in European history. Although this was the end of the old French monarchy, a new monarchy, modeled after the ancient Roman emperors, was briefly established by Napoléon in 1799.

On July 14, 1789, an angry mob of French peasants forced its way into the Bastille, a prison where the king held political prisoners. The mob released the prisoners and destroyed the building. This engraving by Jean-Pierre Houel portrays that event, which is known as the storming of the Bastille.

Monarchy Fades

With the nineteenth century came the Industrial Revolution. Huge numbers of people moved from the countryside to the cities to work in factories. In contact with new people, places, and ideas, many Europeans began to question the divine right of the monarchs. This led to many upheavals in government structures.

BONAPARTISM

"Bonapartism" is a word used to describe despotism, a government or political system in which a ruler with popular consent exercises absolute power. After the French Revolution, the country disintegrated into anarchy. The people once again looked for a leader who could bring order and stability. They found such a person in Napoléon Bonaparte (1769–1821) who rose from obscurity to military greatness, winning the love of the French people. In 1804, Napoléon crowned himself emperor, overriding the ideals of the Declaration of the Rights of Man and of the Citizen. He was tyrannical, cruel, and overly ambitious. After a series of disastrous defeats trying to conquer Europe, he was defeated for the last time in 1815 at Waterloo. Napoléon was exiled to a small island, where he died.

But while movements toward constitutional rule were on the rise from 1789 to 1917, European colonialism was running rampant around the world, with monarchs squarely at the helm. By 1914, Spain, Germany, England, Holland, France, and Portugal controlled almost half of the world.

Although there were still some popular and effective kings and queens, hereditary monarchy as an institution was beginning to die out. The authority of kings and queens was increasingly replaced by parliaments and elected prime ministers.

By the end of World War I (1914–1917), monarchy as it had been known for much of history, had nearly disappeared in Europe. The Russian Revolution in 1917 brought a violent and bloody end to the reign of the czars. Elsewhere in Europe, the power of monarchs had dwindled to become only symbolic.

Kaiser Wilhelm II of Germany

Kaiser Wilhelm II (reigned 1888–1918) was the last German monarch and a symbol of European imperialist power. Unlike his relatives on the English throne (Queen Victoria was his grandmother), Wilhelm was no mere figurehead. As the most powerful leader in Europe at the turn of the twentieth century, Wilhelm was in an enviable but dangerous position.

One of Wilhelm's first actions in 1890 was to dismiss powerful Chancellor Otto von Bismarck, the man responsible for uniting Germany. He then pursued a foreign policy of aggression toward Russia and France, which placed the security of Germany at great risk.

What the kaiser wanted more than anything was "a place in the sun" for the German people. This meant he wanted more colonies and more power for Germany. His desire for more *weltpolitik*, or political power in the world, fueled the nationalist sentiments of the German people and ultimately led to World War I.

The war was a disaster for the German people and for the kaiser as well. By 1918, Germany had gone from being the top power with an enviable standard of living to a chaotic and demoralized state. Kaiser Wilhelm abdicated his throne in November 1918. The German monarchy was finished.

The Execution of the Russian Czar

After his abdication, Kaiser Wilhelm II went into exile in Holland, where he spent the rest of his life. Holland refused to turn him over to be tried for war crimes at the end of World War I. This photo of him as Germany's crown prince was taken in 1880.

In 1917, near the end of World War I, another monarchy was coming to an end. But this one ended quite differently than Kaiser Wilhelm's. Czar Nicholas II of Russia, who reigned from 1894 to 1917, was a private man who never seemed to hold much interest in being king. Although he was an absolute monarch, he was weak and ineffective. When there was a popular uprising in 1905, he refused to listen to the people or create reforms that would lessen the burdens of the country's destitute population.

During the war with Kaiser Wilhelm's Germany, however, civil war broke out and a group of reformers known as the Bolsheviks, led by Vladimir Lenin, took control of Russia. The Bolsheviks were radicals who thought violent overthrow of the monarchy was better than gradual democratic change. Nicholas was forced to abdicate (give up) the throne, but it was too late. The Bolsheviks captured the entire royal family and confined them to a house in the city of Ekaterinburg.

This 1917 photograph shows a stockade surrounding the house in Ekaterinburg, Russia, where Czar Nicholas, his wife, and their five children *(inset)* were held during the Bolshevik Revolution of 1917. They were accompanied by their family doctor and three attendants.

The czar was an important symbol in Russia, and as long as he was alive, the Bolsheviks would be vulnerable to plans to oust the government and restore the monarchy. Since the czar was related to the royal families of Britain, Germany, and Austria, it was likely that those countries might interfere. There was a possibility that once the war ended, the Western powers would send troops to liberate the imprisoned czar with the intention of returning him to his throne. But that wasn't to be. With this fear in mind, the Bolshevik leaders made the decision to execute the entire Russian royal family. In July 1918, the last Russian czar and his family were executed.

Monarchy in the Twenty-first Century

Most of the world's existing monarchies are constitutional monarchies, in which a king or queen reigns but does not rule. A constitutional monarch is recognized as the head of state, but the position is mostly symbolic and ceremonial, and it carries little power. Constitutional monarchies almost always operate within the framework of representative democracy, in which the head of government, usually a prime minister, actually governs the country.

In most constitutional monarchies, the role of the monarch is clearly outlined in the country's written constitution. Significant changes in the rights, power, and responsibilities of these monarchs can be made only by constitutional amendments that can be passed by referendum or weighted majorities in Parliament. Australia, Belgium, Canada, Denmark, Japan, the Netherlands, Norway, Spain, and Sweden are all constitutional monarchies that operate under written constitutions.

The United Kingdom is a constitutional monarchy without a written constitution. As such, the British parliament has the power to change the role of or even abolish the monarchy by passing a law with only a simple majority. Nevertheless, Queen Elizabeth II is arguably the world's most prominent monarch. This is partly because, in addition to ruling the United Kingdom, Queen Elizabeth is the head of state of fifteen countries, including Canada, Australia, New Zealand, and Jamaica. She is also the symbolic head of the commonwealth, a voluntary association of fifty-three states that work to achieve international goals. Moreover, she and her royal family are involved in numerous charities. The queen is patron to more than 3,000 organizations, many of which are outside the United Kingdom.

Other constitutional monarchs spend a lot of time supporting charities, in addition to carrying out their constitutional functions. The Netherlands' popular Queen Beatrix, who is believed to be the second richest woman in the world, shows special interest to issues faced by the disabled. In addition, she is a vigorous supporter of contemporary Dutch art. Spain's Queen Sophia supports various types of medical research, including the study of violence and the treatment of drug addicts. King Albert of Belgium and Britain's Prince Charles support environmental causes.

Queen Elizabeth II of Britain is pictured here waving to onlookers on December 6, 2000, on her way to Parliament to deliver her annual address. One of the world's longest-reigning monarchs, she celebrated her fiftieth anniversary on the throne in 2002.

Today's Absolute Monarchies

There are still a number of traditional monarchies in the world today. Most exist in the Middle East, but the list also includes Bhutan and Brunei in Asia, Swaziland in central Africa, and Tonga in Oceania. The most notable of the absolute monarchies is the Kingdom of Saudi Arabia, where King Fahd has been head of state since 1982. Saudi Arabia has no written constitution, no assembly, and no political parties. King Fahd is both head of state and head of government (prime minister). He rules by decree in accordance with Islamic law and in consultation with a sixty-member cabinet, known as the Consultative Council. King Fahd's brother, Crown Prince Abdullah, is first deputy prime minister and next in line to the throne. It is widely believed that Crown Prince Abdullah has actually been running the government since the king suffered a stroke in 1995.

Although constitutional monarchies by name, Jordan and Morocco are, in effect, absolute monarchies. In Jordan, King Abdallah is both head of state and head of government, and despite the existence of political parties, an appointed senate, and an elected house of representatives, the king has ultimate control over the government and the final word on policy. Morocco, too, has an elected house of representatives. Although King Mohammed VI is not constitutionally the head of government, he has the power to dismiss the prime minister and dissolve the house. He also presides over his appointed cabinet, which makes the country's most important decisions. The Middle East's other absolute monarchies are

Bahrain, Kuwait, Oman, Qatar, and the United Arab Emirates.

The Future of Monarchy

The general trend of the last century indicates a movement away from monarchy—in particular, absolute monarchy—as a viable political system. In the face of international pressure promoting democracy, basic human rights, and increased globalization as a result of the revolution in information technology, even the most absolutist states are slowly and tentatively instituting changes toward greater democracy. In addition, countries such as Australia and Jamaica are actively considering doing away with the monarchal system. Movements supporting the establishment of republics continue to grow in countries that are now constitutional monarchies.

As first deputy prime minister of Saudi Arabia, Crown Prince Abdullah presides over cabinet meetings. He is also commander of the national guard and the kingdom's chief diplomatic representative. Crown Prince Abdullah also takes a leading role in promoting Saudi Arabia's cultural heritage.

TIMELINE

3500 BC	The two kingdoms of Egypt are united.
735– 509 BC	Age of the Roman kings
30 BC	Death of Cleopatra; age of pharaohs ends in Egypt
27 BC	First Roman emperor Octavian
AD 122	Construction of Hadrian's Wall
161– 180	Reign of Marcus Aurelius in Rome
800	Charlemagne is crowned emperor of the Holy Roman Empire.
1066	Battle of Hastings in England
1215	The Magna Carta is signed by King John in England.
1513	Machiavelli's *The Prince* is published in Italy.
1643	Reign of Louis XIV in France
1789	The French Revolution
1888	Reign of Kaiser Wilhelm II in Germany
1918	Nicholas II is executed by the Bolsheviks in Russia.
1952	Queen Elizabeth II of England is crowned.

Page 33: Magna Carta (Excerpt)

1. In the first place we have granted to God, and by this our present charter confirmed for us and our heirs forever that the English Church shall be free, and shall have her rights entire, and her liberties inviolate; and we will that it be thus observed; which is apparent from this that the freedom of elections, which is reckoned most important and very essential to the English Church, we, of our pure and unconstrained will, did grant, and did by our charter confirm and did obtain the ratification of the same from our lord, Pope Innocent III, before the quarrel arose between us and our barons: and this we will observe, and our will is that it be observed in good faith by our heirs forever. We have also granted to all freemen of our kingdom, for us and our heirs forever, all the underwritten liberties, to be had and held by them and their heirs, of us and our heirs forever . . .

9. Neither we nor our bailiffs will seize any land or rent for any debt, as long as the chattels of the debtor are sufficient to repay the debt; nor shall the sureties of the debtor be distrained so long as the principal debtor is able to satisfy the debt; and if the principal debtor shall fail to pay the debt, having nothing wherewith to pay it, then the sureties shall answer for the debt; and let them have the lands and rents of the debtor, if they desire them, until they are indemnified for the debt which they have paid for him, unless the principal debtor can show proof that he is discharged thereof as against the said sureties . . .

40. To no one will we sell, to no one will we refuse or delay, right or justice . . .

63. Wherefore we will and firmly order that the English Church be free, and that the men in our kingdom have and hold all the aforesaid liberties, rights, and concessions, well and peaceably, freely and quietly, fully and wholly, for themselves and their heirs, of us and our heirs, in all respects and in all places forever, as is aforesaid. An oath, moreover, has been taken, as well on our part as on the art of the barons, that all these conditions aforesaid shall be kept in good faith and without evil intent. Given under our hand—the above named and many others being witnesses—in the meadow which is called Runnymede, between Windsor and Staines, on the fifteenth day of June, in the seventeenth year of our reign.

Page 39: The Death Warrant of King Charles I

At the high Co[ur]t of Justice for the tryinge and judginge of Charles Steuart Kinge of England January xxixth Anno D[omi]ni 1648.

Whereas Charles Steuart [King] of England is and standeth convicted [tainted] and condemned of High Treason and other high Crymes, And sentence uppon Saturday last was pronounced against him by this Co[ur]t to be putt to death by the [severing] of his head from his body Of w[hi]ch sentence [execution] yet [remains] to be done, These are therefore to will and require you to see the said sentence executed In the open Streete before Whitehall upon the morrowe being the Thirtieth day of this instante [month] of January betweene the houres of Tenn in the morninge and *Five* in the afternoone of the same day w[i]th full effect And for [so] doing this shall be yo[u]r sufficient warrant And these are to require All Officers and Souldiers and other the good people of this Nation of England to be assistinge unto you in this service Given under o[ur] hands and Seales.

Page 46: The Declaration of the Rights of Man and of the Citizen

Approved by the National Assembly of France, August 26, 1789

The representatives of the French people, organized as a National Assembly, believing that the ignorance, neglect, or contempt of the rights of man are the sole cause of public calamities and of the corruption of governments, have determined to set forth in a solemn declaration the natural, unalienable, and sacred rights of man, in order that this declaration, being constantly before all the members of the Social body, shall remind them continually of their rights and duties; in order that the acts of the legislative power, as well as those of the executive power, may be compared at any moment with the objects and purposes of all political institutions and may thus be more respected, and, lastly, in order that the grievances of the citizens, based hereafter upon simple and incontestable principles, shall tend to the maintenance of the constitution and redound to the happiness of all. Therefore the National Assembly recognizes and proclaims, in the presence and under the auspices of the Supreme Being, the following rights of man and of the citizen:

Articles:

1. Men are born and remain free and equal in rights. Social distinctions may be founded only upon the general good.
2. The aim of all political association is the preservation of the natural and imprescriptible rights of man. These rights are liberty, property, security, and resistance to oppression.
3. The principle of all sovereignty resides essentially in the nation. No body nor individual may exercise any authority which does not proceed directly from the nation.
4. Liberty consists in the freedom to do everything which injures no one else; hence the exercise of the natural rights of each man has no limits except those which assure to the other members of the society the enjoyment of the same rights. These limits can only be determined by law . . .
7. No person shall be accused, arrested, or imprisoned except in the cases and according to the forms prescribed by law. Any one soliciting, transmitting, executing, or causing to be executed, any arbitrary order, shall be punished. But any citizen summoned or arrested in virtue of the law shall submit without delay, as resistance constitutes an offense . . .
9. As all persons are held innocent until they shall have been declared guilty, if arrest shall be deemed indispensable, all harshness not essential to the securing of the prisoner's person shall be severely repressed by law . . .
11. The free communication of ideas and opinions is one of the most precious of the rights of man. Every citizen may, accordingly, speak, write, and print with freedom, but shall be responsible for such abuses of this freedom as shall be defined by law . . .
17. Since property is an inviolable and sacred right, no one shall be deprived thereof except where public necessity, legally determined, shall clearly demand it, and then only on condition that the owner shall have been previously and equitably indemnified.

GLOSSARY

annals A long record of events arranged by year.

anoint To apply oil during a religious ceremony as a sign of sanctification or consecration.

basalt A hard, dense, dark igneous rock that often has a glassy appearance.

coronation The act of crowning a monarch.

Crusades A series of military expeditions undertaken by European Christians during the eleventh, twelfth, and thirteenth centuries to recover the Holy Land from the Muslims.

dynasty A succession of rulers from the same family or line.

garrison A military post.

inalienable Incapable of being removed or transferred to another.

Industrial Revolution The period between the late eighteenth and early twentieth century during which many nations underwent a radical transformation from farm-based to factory-based societies.

liberty The right to freedom to engage in certain actions or express certain beliefs without control or interference from the government.

papyrus An early paper made from the pith, or stems, of an aquatic plant. Used especially by the ancient Egyptians, Greeks, and Romans.

patron Someone who supports, protects, or sponsors someone or something.

Renaissance The period in European history from the fourteenth through the middle of the seventeenth centuries during which there was a revival of classical art, architecture, literature, and learning.

Republic A political system in which the head of state is not a monarch and in which the supreme power lies in a body of citizens who are entitled to elect representatives responsible to them.

Stoicism A way of thinking, or a philosophy, that flourished in ancient Greece in which people felt that, to attain happiness and wisdom, they must restrain their emotions. They refused to show joy or sorrow.

troubadour A twelfth- or thirteenth-century lyric poet in southern France, northern Italy, and northern Spain, who composed and sang songs, often about courtly love.

FOR MORE INFORMATION

Web Sites

Due to the changing nature of Internet links, the Rosen Publishing Group, Inc., has developed an online list of Web sites related to the subject of this book. This site is updated regularly. Please use this link to access the list:

http://www.rosenlinks.com/psps/mono

FOR FURTHER READING

Burns, Khephra. *Mansa Musa: The Lion of Mali*. Orlando: Harcourt, 2001.

Greenblatt, Miriam. *Suleyman the Magnificent and the Ottoman Empire*. Salt Lake City, UT: Benchmark Books, 2002.

Kort, Michael G. *The Handbook of the Middle East*. Breckenridge, CO: Twenty-first Century Books, 2002.

Meltzer, Milton. *In the Days of the Pharaohs: A Look at Ancient Egypt*. New York: Franklin Watts, 2001.

Meltzer, Milton. *Ten Kings and the Worlds They Ruled*. New York: Orchard Books, 2002.

Meltzer, Milton. *Ten Queens: Portraits of Women of Power*. New York: Dutton Books, 1998.

Nelson, Julie. *West African Kingdoms*. Austin, TX: Raintree Steck-Vaughn Publishers, 2002.

Rees, Rosemary. *The Incas*. Barrington, IL: Heinemann Library, 2001.

Severns, Karen. *Hirohito*. Broomall, PA: Chelsea House Publishers, 1988.

Van Loon, Henrik Willem. *The Story of Mankind*. New York: W. W. Norton & Co., 1999.

BIBLIOGRAPHY

Dodson, Aidan. *Monarchs of the Nile*. Cairo, Egypt: The American University in Cairo Press, 2000.

Johnson, Paul. *The Civilization of Ancient Egypt*. New York: HarperCollins, 1999.

MacDonald, Fiona. *Timelines: Kings and Queens*. New York: Franklin Watts, 1995.

Nicolson, Harold. *Kings, Courts, and Monarchy*. New York: Simon & Schuster, 1962.

Shaw, Ian, ed. *The Oxford History of Ancient Egypt*. New York: Oxford University Press, 2000.

INDEX

PHOTO CREDITS

Cover, p. 17 © Bettmann/Corbis; back cover (top left) NARA; back cover (all others) © The 2000 Nova Corporation; pp. 4–5 © Colin McPherson/Corbis; p. 8 © Hulton/Archive/Getty Images; p. 10 © Lauros/Giraudon/Bridgeman Art Library; pp. 13, 25 © Scala/Art Resource, NY; pp. 14, 28, 29, 32, 47 © Gianni Dagli Orti; p. 16 © Alinari/Art Resource, NY; p. 19 © AKG London/Erich Lessing; p. 21 © Sean Sexton Collection/Corbis; pp. 21 (inset), 24 © Erich Lessing/Art Resource, NY; p. 23 © Joe Cornish Photography; p. 26 © Bridgeman Art Library, London/SuperStock; p. 31 © AKG-images/Erich Lessing; p. 33 U.S. National Archives & Records Administration; p. 34 © Ludovic Maisabt/Corbis; pp. 35, 41, 45 Library of Congress Prints and Photographs Division, Washington, D.C.; p. 36 © Bridgeman Art Library; p. 37 © National Portrait Gallery, London/SuperStock; p. 39 The United Kingdom Parliament/House of Lords Record Office; p. 43 © Hulton-Deutsh Collection/ Corbis; p. 46 © Musée de la Révolution Française, Visille, France/Bridgeman Art Library; p. 50 © Henry Guttmann/Hulton Archive/Getty Images; p. 51 © Corbis; p. 51 (inset) New York World-Telegram and the Sun Newspaper Photograph Collection (Library of Congress); p. 53 © Max Nash/AP/Wide World Photos; p. 55 © European Press Photo Agency, EPA/AP Wide World Photos.

ABOUT THE AUTHOR

Katy Schiel is a writer and artist who lives in the Boston area with her husband and two cats. She studied history at the University of Massachusetts at Amherst after spending a few years wandering through Europe.

Designer: Nelson Sá; **Editor:** Wayne Anderson;
Photo Researcher: Hillary Arnold